A spiritual journey Of findi
The Woman

A Queen Of A

Woman

Poetry Chapbook

Chanel Ny'eema Person

Contents

Healing

She Endured pain

She felt

She cried

She ignored

She suppressed the truth

For temporary relief

She carried secrets

In the bags of her eyes

Cycles of generational

shame and family hurt

Rained on her heart

She was a born leader

Unaware of her strength

Yet her siblings saw her as so

She fought and

Finally let go,

The past was set free from her

Burden of restraint

She reclaimed her freedom

Starting with the reflection in the mirror

She felt God's touch

With signs of relief

Appearing in her life

She felt alone

Yet she knew she wasn't

The universe spoke

And she understood

The Queen in her was awakened

Yet work still needed to be done

The little girl in her cried

Out for her dreams to be fulfilled

She was in need of protection

During this time of growing pains

Her Guardian angels led

Her along the way in synchronicity

Numbers were her best friend as it advised

Her down her path

She Questioned the people

In her life so she disconnected

to form and become who she knew she was

Friends were few

But God was plenty

In this time

She grew well

She grew new

She grew wise

She grew strong like

The roots that was planted

Within her kindred soul

Chanel Ny'eema Person

She was aligned with purpose

Now she speaks with clarity

Love

She met the masculine reflection

Of her soul, her twin flame

It was pretty insane

A soul-mate beyond

Soul-mates

A holy-grail connection

The first kiss sent surges

Through our bodies like energy

Out of control

Our heart's touched that night

Awakening our souls cry through

Our gazing eyes in between kisses

Longing for each other

Like we met before in past life

A moment of familiarity that felt

Like home

Then seperation occurred

Causing curiosity and confusion

Of the unknown between our intense

Connection

It was something close to perfection

In departure

They battled and loved

To only get a glimpse of what God

Could of Had for them over the horizon

It Ended before it began

A moment remembered Forever

Awakening

This moment ignited

The Queen in her

Beautiful as light striking

Through her pores within

She stood tall and gracious

like the wise tree that she is compared to

She overcame great challenging
heights like the everest mountain that
touched the bright skies of wondering winds

God made creating fun for her

As she blurred the past, she was reminded

Of her wisdom

Her mind was as beautiful

As the colors in the rainbow

She was surrounded by the authenticity

Of her aura

Her grace pulled you in like

Gravity from the depth of her soul

Over the waves of vibrant energy

She was able to reach people

Through questions of purpose

Uplifting in value

Ideas appeared in her dreams

That were unknown to her reality

Gifts of visions wrapped

In truth that was ignored

With her conscious being

She understood in those

Moments she was being showed

Freedom of mind

Soaring through the sky
Of unlimited life, feeling
Alive and loving forever as
A strong Queen

She wore confidence like

A luxurious gown dripped of Gold

Beaded in love

Her kinky hair

Creative by day

Wrapped and tucked in by night

souring with volume and beauty

Like a melanin toned

Art piece

Her skin glistened in the sun

Her melting caramel

Brown eyes like almond coffee

Brightens your every morning

A Queen Of A Woman

She has womanly curves

Passed her hips

balanced

By her navel

She smiles with grace

Yet winks with sass

Fixated on vision

She can stare life

Right into you like

Red lazors heating your heart

She gives you a feeling you

Thought never existed

A feeling of light within

Her presence is of vibrant

Peace accompanied with

A bright colorful aura

She is a Queen shaped into a

Being of intention

Your lover

Your heart

Created in human form

Chanel Ny'eema Person

She is an artistic soul

Maneuvering around life

Trying to piece together

The world and it's art

The art in her heart

Was different from any other

She was a unique fingerprint

Of the universe

Godfidence

She was ready to heal the

Impaired world with her spirit of wisdom

The essence of her kinky twist out

Curls was confidence not defined by gravity

Her curls stood tall

Like the crown she styled daily

My handsome man who is worthy

Of this Queen .. Her Beauty is not cracked easily

She is filled with love and compassion

For the world that surrounds her lively experience

She has strength that she bares and

Grew accustomed to building armor of

Melanin too strong for even the sun to get

Through

Her words are medicine to his ego
That questions his insecurity of masculinity

She now attracts men that equal

Her love and cancel out ego

She did her time and healing

Fighting away her she-go

Her insecurities floated away

With her past no longer in existence

She unraveled her past and

Dissected her wounds to heal

Beauty

She now lives with abundant joy

And a smile that gives life

Everyday she elude's herself

In nature sinking into peace

She welcome's herself everyday

To live life gracefully

She understands that love keeps the skin young

Protect the skin that protects your
soulful existence

How do we determine true beauty when
We all have the same parts that make
up a face?

We should not be defined by our faces

But rather our energy of being

Replication of love and fear

Together is non-existent

Time stands still in the

Midst of being yourself

I will not be defined by my symmetrical face

But my aura of existence dipped in character

And sparked by charisma

Become a spiritual masterpiece

Unafraid to exist within and to emanate without

Understand the architect of your body and how

Far it can take you

Let unconditional love peak your
Mental capacity of supreme virtue

Fulfillment

God held her hand as her

Mind developed in wisdom

Unafraid to learn of herself

Her voice grew louder

Time stopped as she

Grew ahead of her time

Her signature of truth began

To imprint on other's hearts

She was benevolent beyond

Her demise , while the affection

showed in her eyes

She surrounded herself with the elite
Joy of love engulfing the beautiful
Sacredness of being
She was aware of intense awakening
Aligning her steps with visions of clarity
Sent from high above

Her mind was arched and arrowed to God

With purpose as her target

She listened to the light

Of her firing desire forged

From her soul

She began to master the tranquility

Of natural thought behind the mask

Of she-go

She now matched the power that

Was evolving inside of her

Peace

Her love for herself portrayed on the world

She laughed and smiled

Through the growing pains to excellence

She humbled herself to her knees

To grow in faith daily

Her essence was a fresh

Soulful sound to her melodic rhythm

She danced by the ocean to

The rhythm of her pretty thoughts

Surrounding her curiosity

Of life's beauty has to offer

Connecting with other dimensions

Of her godly self

Same moment, different world

She felt like it was blissful deja-vu

Sitting pretty is an understatement

She is filtering her thoughts through the

Positive realms of the mind affirming

The truths of her future

Focused in on the nature

That surrounds her

Highly aware of the divine

Signs God sends her daily

Her godly grace leaves you with a lasting
Love aftertaste with a trace of familiarity from
the soul

Her skin regimen was pure love

Love of God

Love of Self

Love of Others

Love keeps the skin young, unconditionally

Reflecting inner power

She expressed herself through art

Of creative thought crafted by her heart

She's dripped in vulnerability draped with
strength
Upon her shoulders of experience
exuding knowledge
Of the wise

She learns her purpose is greater

Than she is and is being nudged by

Her ancestors that are whispering

Love in her ear to claim her throne and

Become the healer that her presence exudes

Her plethora is of rich cashmere silk

Beyond sound

Beyond touch

Beyond taste

Free of self

Life was as beautiful as

The diapason in her voice

Flowing from her sharp tongue

Of bearing fresh fruit

As her spirit was being led

She asked God with grace to

Guide my hands

Guide my voice

Guide my mind

To speak truth into people's lives

For this was her purpose fulfilled

God used her as she

Stepped out of herself and spoke loud in faith

She felt free and finally understood

The power of love

Chills surrounded her as she felt

The presence of God in her life

She cried tears of joy and relief

For she was never alone

A young queen that was unaware of her strength due to her environment and lack of focus to understand her cause to purpose. Her lack of wisdom of truth led her astray to insecure thoughts feeling less than what she knew God saw her to be. She overcame anxiety and indecision through spiritual healing. A journey that is only walked with God and herself to understand her reason to be alive and how to give life to others in whichever way that may be for you. She understood the power of self reflection, positive thinking and letting go. Most importantly she understood the power of prayer to guide her footsteps to a higher calling and to uplift her voice to speak and be heard for who she was meant to be authentically. That woman was A Queen Of A Woman with purpose and a voice of power and faith. Her Godly confidence led her to write her story through poetry to lead by example and show her greatness to the world.

To transform young girls and woman growing into Queens by loving themselves unconditionally and understanding the power that they have to shake the world on purpose with the presence of God shining in their lives.

To a Future Queen (SELF)

Made in the USA
Middletown, DE
06 June 2021